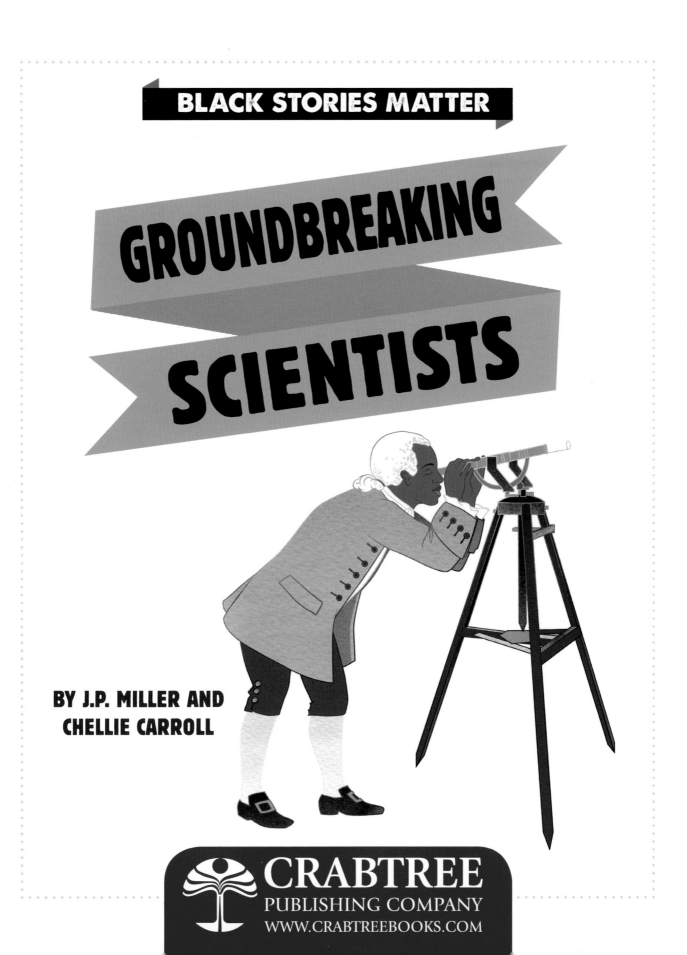

BLACK STORIES MATTER

GROUNDBREAKING
SCIENTISTS

**BY J.P. MILLER AND
CHELLIE CARROLL**

CRABTREE
PUBLISHING COMPANY
WWW.CRABTREEBOOKS.COM

CRABTREE
PUBLISHING COMPANY
WWW.CRABTREEBOOKS.COM

Author: J.P. Miller

Editorial director: Kathy Middleton

Series editor: Julia Bird

Editor: Ellen Rodger

Designer: Peter Scoulding

Artist: Chellie Carroll

Proofreader: Petrice Custance

**Production coordinator and
    Prepress technician:** Tammy McGarr

Print coordinator: Katherine Berti

Library and Archives Canada Cataloguing in Publication

Title: Groundbreaking scientists / by J.P. Miller and Chellie Carroll.
Names: Miller, J. P. (Janice P.), author. | Carroll, Chellie, illustrator.
Description: Series statement: Black stories matter | Illustrated by
  Chellie Carroll. | Originally published: London : Wayland, 2020. |
  Includes bibliographical references and index.
Identifiers: Canadiana (print) 20200370960 |
  Canadiana (ebook) 20200371096 |
  ISBN 9781427128096 (hardcover) |
  ISBN 9781427128133 (softcover) |
  ISBN 9781427128171 (HTML)
Subjects: LCSH: Scientists, Black—Biography—Juvenile literature. |
  LCGFT: Biographies.
Classification: LCC Q141 .M55 2021 | DDC j509.2/396—dc23

Library of Congress Cataloging-in-Publication Data

Names: Miller, J. P. (Janice P.), author. | Carroll, Chellie, illustrator.
Title: Groundbreaking scientists / by J.P. Miller and Chellie Carroll.
Description: New York, NY : Crabtree Publishing Company, 2021.
  Series: Black stories matter |
  Includes bibliographical references and index.
Identifiers: LCCN 2020048118 (print) | LCCN 2020048119 (ebook) |
  ISBN 9781427128096 (hardcover) |
  ISBN 9781427128133 (paperback) |
  ISBN 9781427128171 (ebook)
Subjects: LCSH: African American scientists--Biography--
  Juvenile literature. | African American inventors--Biography--
  Juvenile literature. | African American psychologists--Biography--
  Juvenile literature.
Classification: LCC Q141 .M49 2021 (print) | LCC Q141 (ebook) |
  DDC 509.2/2--dc23
LC record available at https://lccn.loc.gov/2020048118
LC ebook record available at https://lccn.loc.gov/2020048119

Crabtree Publishing Company
www.crabtreebooks.com   1-800-387-7650

Published in 2021 by Crabtree Publishing Company

Published in Canada
Crabtree Publishing
616 Welland Ave.
St. Catharines, Ontario
L2M 5V6

Published in the United States
Crabtree Publishing
347 Fifth Avenue
Suite 1402–145
New York, NY 10016

Printed in the U.S.A./022021/CG20201123

CONTENTS

BENJAMIN BANNEKER

IF MEMORY SERVES ME

The movement was barely noticeable. Benjamin Banneker stared at the pocket watch his friend had lent him.
Tick-tock.
Tick-tock.
Tick-tock.
Time was ticking away. Benjamin held the watch to his ear. He was curious about how it worked.

Benjamin flipped the pocket watch over and popped open its back. Tiny wheels and springs moved about. He focused on how they worked together and committed it to memory.

Long after Benjamin Banneker returned the pocket watch, the image of its inner workings stayed in his mind.

If memory serves me ….

Benjamin was confident he could build a working clock—and he did.

At the age of 20, Benjamin made a wooden clock that chimed every hour on the hour.

BORN:
November 9, 1731–
October 9, 1806

NATIONALITY:
American

OCCUPATION:
Surveyor, inventor, farmer, writer

The son of a free Black woman and a formerly enslaved Black man, Benjamin grew up free on his parents' small tobacco farm. Despite little schooling, he showed an early talent for math, science, and **astronomy**.

Benjamin's talents came to the attention of some wealthy neighbors, the Ellicotts, who moved nearby in 1771. They encouraged his studies, particularly of astronomy, lending him books and equipment.

In 1790, President George Washington gained permission to build a new capital city along the Potomac River. This would become Washington, D.C. , the center of government as well as the location of the White House—the home for each elected president of the United States.

Andrew Ellicott, Benjamin's neighbor and a cousin of George Washington, was hired to help survey and map out the site. Andrew asked Benjamin to help him with this work, and together they measured out the boundaries of the new capital city.

Benjamin also had a good understanding of farming from growing up on his parents' tobacco farm and living in a farming community. So, on his return from Washington, D.C., he decided to use his skills to help his fellow farmers.

It wasn't easy for a Black person to get a book published in Benjamin's day, but he overcame the odds. In 1791, Benjamin wrote and published the first of several almanacs for farmers. It was filled with weather predictions, farming tips, and even some helpful medical advice. He went on to publish an almanac for each of the next six years.

Benjamin went on to become a respected scientist and **innovator**.

He saw his new status as an opportunity to address the ongoing **injustice** of slavery and the treatment of Blacks by Whites. As proof of his abilities, Benjamin sent a copy of his almanac to the U.S. Secretary of State, Thomas Jefferson, along with a letter in which he said:

> "I freely and cheerfully acknowledge, that
> I am of the African race, and that color
> which is natural to them of the deepest dye ..."

Jefferson, a slave-owner and Founding Father of the United States, would later become president. Benjamin urged him to end the ongoing pain and injustice of slavery and to begin to consider Blacks as equal to Whites. He also respectfully pointed out that the country had gone to war to gain independence from Britain, but continued to keep Black people as slaves.

Benjamin died at home in 1806, aged 74. On the day of his funeral, his house burned down, destroying most of his papers and possessions, including his copies of the almanacs. Despite this, Benjamin is still remembered today as one of the first notable early African-American **intellectuals** and scientists.

DR. SEGENET KELEMU

THE DAY OF THE LOCUSTS

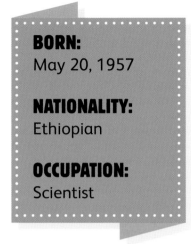

BORN:
May 20, 1957

NATIONALITY:
Ethiopian

OCCUPATION:
Scientist

The sound of a million tiny wings flapping could be heard long before they were seen. The locusts were on their way to the town of Finote Selam in Ethiopia. There was nothing anyone could do to stop them.

Segenet Kelemu was just a child, but the day of the locust swarm changed her life forever. She watched from the village home where she lived with her family as the swarm of locusts feasted on their crops. Like all the villagers, her parents relied on the crops to feed their family and to sell for money. The swarm destroyed everything.

Famine spread throughout the land and crop failures led to starvation and sickness. Segenet was shocked and saddened by the events. For the first time, she saw for herself something bigger than life in the small town of Finote Selam.

Segenet decided not to follow tradition or **customs**. She wanted more for her life than an early, **arranged marriage**. She wanted to improve **agriculture** in Africa.

> "If you don't have food, then everything else is irrelevant."

In 1974, Segenet packed her things and left home to attend Addis Ababa University in Ethiopia's capital city, where she studied agriculture. She was the first woman in her area to go to university.

Greenhouses filled with plants and insects became Segenet's new home. She became an expert on plant diseases. Her work led her to further her studies at university in the U.S. and all over the world.

In 2006, China honored Segenet with their Friendship Award. It was their highest honor for a foreign expert, awarded for making exceptional contributions to China's economic and social progress.

As Segenet crossed the stage to receive her award, she wanted to shrink smaller and smaller with each step:

> "As I was handed a gold medal by the president of China, I felt very embarrassed as they read out all the things I had done. I thought: Here I am from a dirt-poor country in Africa, and I'm making a difference in China."

A voice in Segenet's head told her to think about moving back home, where she could help solve the problems in her own area of the world.

The voice grew louder and more insistent. In 2007, Segenet and her family decided to move to Kenya, where Segenet became head of an international research center dedicated to investigating which crops to grow where and when, and how to protect crops from insects, such as locusts.

Segenet is part of a new generation of scientists passionate about improving agriculture in Africa and using their work to help fight poverty, hunger, and disease.

DR. MAGGIE ADERIN-POCOCK

STARGAZER

As far as young Maggie Aderin was concerned, the debate was over. There was life in outer space, and *The Clangers* television show proved it! The fictional mouse family that lived on a distant planet inspired her lifelong love for space research.

BORN:
March 9, 1968

NATIONALITY:
British

OCCUPATION:
Space scientist

Maggie grew up in north London, the daughter of Nigerian parents who divorced when she was four. She moved house 13 times during her childhood, but one thing that stayed the same was the night sky. Born a year before the first human set foot on the Moon in 1969, Maggie was not the only person to dream of being an astronaut at a time of many space missions.

The dream of space exploration inspired Maggie to work hard at school. She even built her own telescope when she was a teenager. But school was a struggle for Maggie.

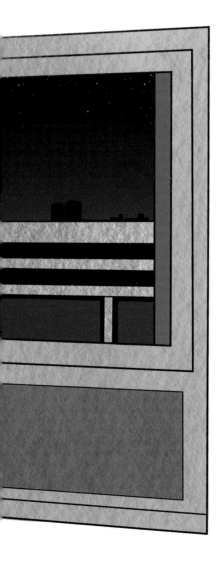

"My problem with education was that I had **dyslexia** so I found reading and writing quite difficult."

Some of her teachers doubted that Maggie could ever become a scientist. Scientific study was dominated by White men. At times, Maggie also doubted herself. But her parents' encouragement kept her going.

After she completed a Master's degree in physics and a **PhD** in mechanical engineering, Maggie worked at Britain's Ministry of Defence. Imagine her hanging from the door of a plane photographing missiles in the air underneath her. Although she felt a bit like a fictional secret agent, Maggie loved her job helping to construct a missile warning system.

Maggie's next assignment for the government was equally dangerous. Many hidden landmines are left behind after wars, and they can hurt people when they explode. Maggie helped develop detectors to find the mines so they could be deactivated and made safe.

Maggie's work hasn't yet taken her into space, although it remains one of her dreams. For now, her work on huge space instruments, such as the telescopes at the Gemini Observatory in Chile, is the closest she has got to reaching the stars.

> "Every night they opened up the telescope dome just as the Sun was setting and the stars would boldly appear."

Maggie keeps on stargazing. In 2014, she became the cohost of the British television show, *The Sky at Night.* This brought her passion for space to a new audience. She also runs an educational company and makes regular visits to schools to educate and inspire young people. She wants them—and especially young girls—to take an interest in science.

GEORGE WASHINGTON CARVER

SERVING THE LAND

BORN: c. 1865–
January 5, 1943

NATIONALITY:
American

OCCUPATION:
Agricultural scientist

Life presented some big challenges to young George Washington Carver. Born enslaved in Missouri, he was orphaned at a young age. George was often sick as a child and could not do hard farm labor. He did household chores instead and taught himself about the natural world around him.

George and his brother were brought up by the farmers who had owned their mother. They received a basic education and both learned how to read and write.

Young George loved to be outdoors. He would go to his favorite spot on the Carver farm and stay there for hours, exploring nature and working in his secret garden—digging, planting, and talking to his crops.

George was a gifted gardener. Neighbors started to call him "the plant doctor." He decided to follow his passion and study agriculture at university.

But George was refused a place by many schools. Then, when he was finally accepted at Highland University in Kansas, as soon as the university learned he was Black, they said they had made a mistake and turned him away.

George was determined. He took over some land in Kansas and started planting different plants and crops, carrying out his own experiments and learning through his work. He also studied music and art at university for a year. He was eventually awarded a spot at Iowa State Agricultural College to study plant science.

After George graduated, Booker T. Washington, a prominant Black leader and founder of the leading Black university, Tuskegee Institute in Alabama, offered him a job. George was already teaching at Iowa State Agricultural College—the first Black person to do so in the college's history.

Once George heard of Booker's offer, he didn't hesitate. He believed it was his destiny to help the farmers of Alabama.

George arrived in Alabama ready to work. He found an old horse-drawn wagon and filled it with farm equipment. He took his mobile classroom out to the farmers.

The first lesson George taught was the importance of growing different crops in a field each year to keep the soil rich and **fertile**.

"Where the soil is rich, the people flourish, physically and economically."

George showed farmers how to plant and harvest sweet potatoes. Where the soil was worn out from constantly growing cotton plants, George encouraged farmers to plant crops such as black-eyed peas, peanuts, and soya beans. These would help put goodness back into the soil. The crops also produced food that could feed farmers' families.

But George didn't stop there. He set up a laboratory to help find other uses for the new crops. Over time, George and his assistants found hundreds of new uses for the humble peanut, such as being used to make shampoo and shaving cream!

George's fame as a scientist spread throughout the country. He also became known as a campaigner for equality between races. All of this attracted White **conservationists** and young Black geniuses to Tuskegee Institute. George received offers of work from all over the world, but opted to stay at Tuskegee for his whole life.

Thanks to his faith and hard work, George Washington Carver rose from slavery to become one of the most prominent agricultural scientists in the world.

DR. MAE JEMISON

SPACE DREAMER

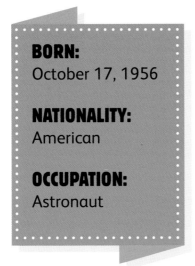

BORN:
October 17, 1956

NATIONALITY:
American

OCCUPATION:
Astronaut

Dr. Mae Jemison was working as a doctor when she heard that the Johnson Space Center in Houston, Texas was recruiting people to train as astronauts. Her heart racing, Mae picked up the phone. This was her big chance.

"Johnson Space Center, how may I direct your call?"

"I would like to apply for your astronaut program."

Mae braced herself to hear laughter come from the other end of the phone. Instead, the receptionist simply replied: "Okay, I'll transfer you to the Astronaut Selection Office."

After she had recovered from the shock, Mae quickly gave her address to the person on the other end of the line. Days later, the application arrived.

When Mae was growing up, she dreamed of becoming an astronaut. People tried to talk Mae out of her dream, giving her all sorts of reasons girls could not go into space. She never believed them. Instead, Mae found out everything she could about the National Space and Aeronautics Administration (NASA) **Apollo program** and worked very hard at school.

> ## "I always believed that I would go into space."

Mae had already accomplished some amazing things in her 30-plus years before she made that telephone call to the Johnson Space Center.

She had studied for a degree in chemical engineering at Stanford University in California. She also studied medicine and became a doctor. She worked in West Africa for two years, providing medical care and researching **vaccines**. She then started a practice as a family doctor in Los Angeles.

But all along, her childhood dream of becoming an astronaut stayed with her.

Out of over 2,000 applicants, Mae and 14 other people were chosen for NASA's astronaut training program. She reported to Houston on June 4, 1987, ready for five years of the most rigorous training imaginable.

On September 12, 1992, all the main TV stations in the U.S. had their cameras focused on Launch Pad 39B at the Kennedy Space Center in Florida. Mae Jemison was one of seven crew members ready for takeoff inside the space shuttle *Endeavour*. She was to become the first African-American woman to fly into space. Her role: to carry out bone cell research and other experiments.

"I didn't even think about being the first African-American woman in space .... I just wanted to go to space."

Eight days and more than 3 million miles (5 million km) later, Mae returned to Earth a happy, but changed person. "The experience made me feel very connected with the universe … My being was just as much a part of the universe as any star or comet."

DRS. KENNETH & MAMIE CLARK

HOW DOLLS HELPED END SEGREGATION

One by one, the Black children were led into the room. On a table were two dolls with identical features, but one doll was dark-skinned, and the other doll was white.

BORN:
Kenneth: July 14, 1914–
May 1, 2005
Mamie: April 18, 1917–
August 11, 1983

NATIONALITY: American

OCCUPATION:
Psychologists

Each child was asked the same questions. They were instructed to point at, pick up, or describe the doll they believed best answered the question.
"What do you see?"
"A black doll and a white doll."

"Which is the nice doll?"
The child points to the white doll.

"Why is the white doll the nice doll?"
"Because he's white."
"Which doll is the mean doll?"

The child touches the black doll. "Him."

"Why is the black doll the mean doll?"

"Because he's black."
The questions varied.
Which doll is pretty?
Which doll is ugly?
Which doll is good?
Which doll do you want to play with?

The negative feelings toward the black doll remained the same.

Each "Doll Test" ended with the child being asked to identify the doll that looked most like them. The children all chose the black doll. Most were reluctant to do so. Others became emotional. Some even stormed out of the room in anger.

Dr. Kenneth Clark explained the children's behavior:

22

> "They were emotionally upset at having to identify with the doll that they had rejected."

Kenneth and Mamie Clark met as students at Howard University in Washington, D.C. They were filled with hopes and dreams for a brighter future. They recognized early on that education was key to achieving this. They followed each other to Columbia University and were the first and second African Americans to earn a PhD in psychology in the university's history.

The Doll Test was first invented by Mamie as part of her university degree. As trained psychologists, Kenneth and Mamie developed the test with the aim of showing the lasting damage on Black children of educating Black and White children in separate schools.

They performed the Doll Test on 160 children between the ages of three and seven during the 1940s.

The results showed that children repeatedly thought better of the white doll than the black doll. They concluded that: "**prejudice**, **discrimination**, and **segregation**" created a feeling of **inferiority** among Black children and damaged their self-esteem.

At the time of the Doll Test, the Clarks could have no idea that 15 years later it would be important in overturning the laws that segregated schools in the U.S.

In 1951, Oliver Brown took the Kansas Board of Education to court for denying a place at an all-White school to his daughter, Linda. At a later trial, Kenneth Clark's report helped convince the Supreme Court that separate schools were not equal and that segregation was unfairly damaging to Black students.

Kenneth and Mamie remained committed to equal educational opportunities for Black children. They were co-founders of Harlem Youth Opportunities Unlimited (HARYOU), which focuses on achieving this goal for young people in Harlem, New York.

Kenneth and Mamie Clark also continued their psychological research. They performed many more studies on **racial identification** among Black children. The enormous impact of the Doll Test is still felt today.

The New York Times.

HIGH COURTS END SCHOOL SEGREGATION

DR. PATRICIA BATH

20/20 VISION

"Doctor, my vision is blurred."
"Doctor, I see halos
around lights at night."
"Doctor, I can't see!"

BORN:
November 4, 1942–
May 30, 2019

NATIONALITY:
American

OCCUPATION:
Ophthalmologist

As a student ophthalmologist, or eye doctor, Dr. Patricia Bath had studied every eye condition imaginable. Now, she was an intern at the Harlem Hospital Center in New York.

Immediately, Patricia noticed the contrast in the number of people with sight problems at the Harlem Hospital, where most of the patients were Black, compared to the eye clinic at Columbia University, where patients were mostly White. She estimated that around twice as many Black people were suffering from vision loss than White people.

This troubled Patricia. Harlem was her home; these people were her people. So Patricia resolved to find the best treatment for people with eye conditions, not just among the Black community, but everywhere.

This determination was typical of Patricia. Her sights were set on doing her best even when she was just a teenager.

"Eyesight is a basic right."

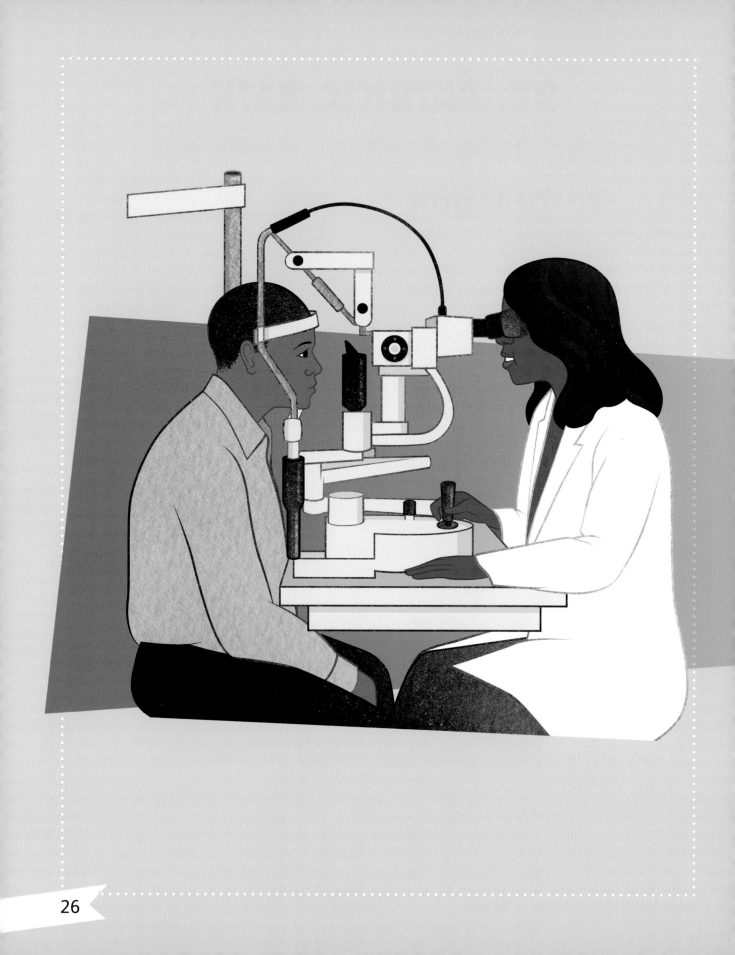

At school, Patricia had excelled in math and science. In high school, she won a National Science Foundation **Scholarship**. This allowed her to study the connections between cancer, nutrition, and stress at Yeshiva University in New York.

While at Yeshiva, Patricia discovered a math **equation** that could predict cancer growth. That was a pretty significant accomplishment for a teenager. The young genius was recognized for her discovery at the International Fifth Congress of Nutrition.

Patricia graduated from Howard University in 1968. By then, her focus was clearly on research. She was determined to find ways for everyone to have 20/20 vision and healthy eyes. She was not seeking to be the first in anything, but she managed to do just that.

In 1981, Patricia got her breakthrough when she invented the Laserphaco Probe. The probe was the first to use a laser to remove cataracts, which are cloudy growths on the eye that impair vision. Patricia would later become the first to perform cataract surgery using her new invention.

"It's only when history looks back that you realize that you were the first. I was not seeking to be the first, I was seeking to do my thing (job)."

The invention of the Laserphaco Probe also made Patricia the first Black woman doctor to receive a United States **patent** in the field of medicine.

Not everyone celebrated Patricia's success. Some were upset. Angry even. Jealousy would not allow some to accept that the petite Black woman from the inner city had made such an incredible contribution to the field of ophthalmology. Patricia did not listen to their negativity.

"I did not allow that to phase my vision. If anything, it challenged and inspired me not to be equal, but to be better and the best."

In all, there are now five U.S. patents in Patricia's name. She has received numerous awards and honors over the years for her contributions to medicine. In 1999, the Smithsonian Museum in Washington included Patricia in its Innovative Lives Exhibition and Program. In 2009, President Barack Obama appointed her to his commission on digital accessibility for the blind. This led to regulations aimed at helping blind people access new and better technologies for computers, televisions, and phones.

DR. DANIEL HALE WILLIAMS

A WORK OF HEART

The year was 1893. The hospital doors burst open and slammed against the walls. The staff of Provident Hospital in Chicago jumped into action. Chief Surgeon, Dr. Daniel Hale Williams, examined the patient.

BORN:
January 18, 1856–
August 4, 1931

NATIONALITY:
American

OCCUPATION:
Surgeon

He did not like what he saw. The patient was an unresponsive Black man in his 20s. He had been stabbed in the chest during a fight. Daniel observed that there was almost no bleeding. That meant that the injury went much deeper.

Daniel examined the patient's heart. He discovered that a major blood vessel had been cut. It would take some work, but he believed that he could repair it.

Most doctors and surgeons were against open-heart surgery at that time. It was just too risky. Daniel had to make a quick decision in order to save the man's life.

Daniel made a small cut in the patient's chest with a **scalpel**. First he repaired a cut to an artery. Then he carefully sewed up the patient's pericardium, the sac

that surrounds the heart. He and his team now faced an anxious wait to see if the patient would recover.

Fifty-one days later, the patient, James Cornish, walked out of Provident Hospital. He would live for another 20 years. Dr. Daniel Hale Williams had made his mark on history as the first surgeon to perform open-heart surgery.

In 1894, after hearing of Daniel's work, President Grover Cleveland made him Chief Surgeon at Freedmen's Hospital (now Howard University Hospital) in Washington, D.C. He wanted Daniel to make the same changes at Freedmen's Hospital that Daniel had already made at Provident Hospital. Daniel accepted the challenge and set to work.

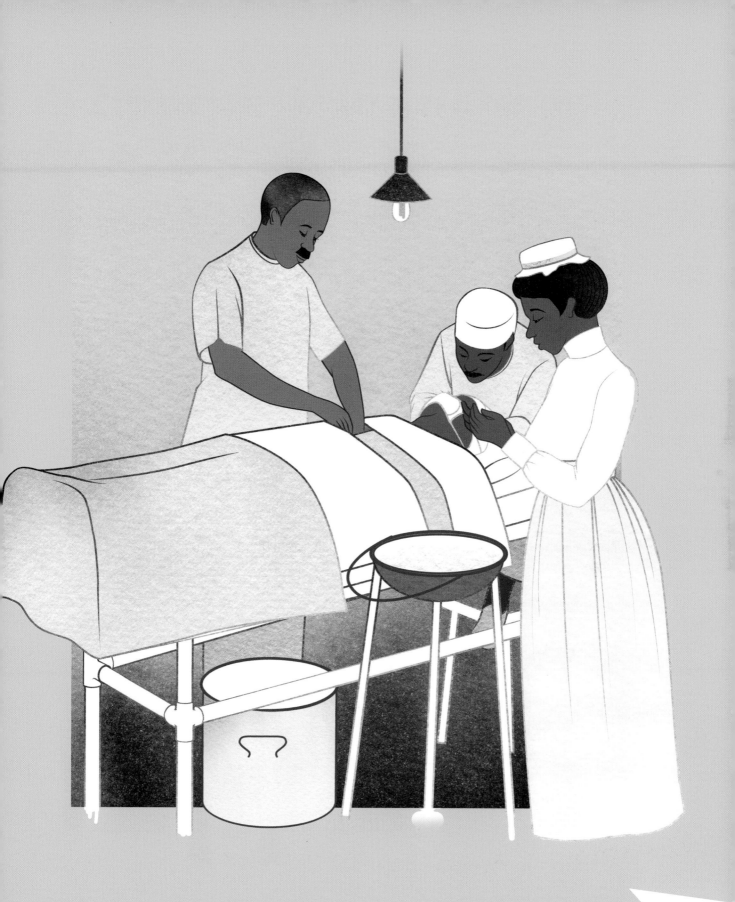

Patient care came first and foremost. Daniel trained the staff in how to **sterilize** surgical instruments. And just as had happened at Provident Hospital, patient infections quickly dropped. He established training schools for Black doctors and nurses at the hospital.

The Freedmen's Hospital was improving fast under Daniel's direction, but this did not convince the White citizens of Washington, D.C. to use the hospital. They were not convinced that a Black surgeon was as capable of caring for them as a White surgeon.

Four years later, in 1898, Daniel returned to Provident Hospital. He also worked in other hospitals over his long career. Daniel performed hundreds of open-heart surgeries and all but eight were successful. In 1913, in recognition of his achievements, he became the first Black man to be accepted into the American College of Surgeons.

"A people who don't make provision for their own sick and suffering are not worthy of civilization."

PHILIP EMEAGWALI

THE CONNECTION THAT CHANGED THE WORLD

Philip Emeagwali was just a teenager, but his homeland of Biafra needed him. Nigeria declared war on Biafra in 1967, after Biafra tried to break away and become independent. So Philip became a child soldier, doing his bit for the Biafran forces.

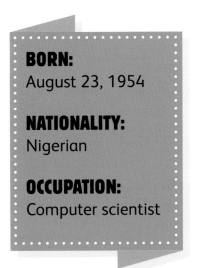

BORN:
August 23, 1954

NATIONALITY:
Nigerian

OCCUPATION:
Computer scientist

For three years there was destruction and famine all around him. Philip managed to survive both.

Before the war, Philip had been an excellent student. After the war, he went back to school but his family couldn't afford to keep him there. Instead, Philip's father taught him everything he could about math and Philip spent his time in the local library, studying. One of Philip's favorite pastimes was solving 100 math problems in an hour!

Philip was soon solving advanced math problems, so his friends nicknamed him "calculus." Philip's incredible math skills won him a scholarship to Oregon State University in Corvallis, Oregon.

As a child, Philip had been fascinated by bees. He noticed that in a colony there were worker bees, drones, and a queen bee. Each had a specific job to do. Philip was most interested in the workmanship of the beehive. The worker bees made the honeycomb into multiple six-sided tubes of wax, or hexagons. From the bees, Philip learned that the hexagon was the most efficient shape for the honeycomb. It used the least amount of wax to build and it could hold more honey.

Philip made a connection between the bees' work and computer science. He believed that if computers could imitate the honeycomb by using the least amount of electronic circuitry to carry out instructions, the computer would be more efficient and powerful.

"It is smarter to borrow from nature than to reinvent the wheel."

To help with his research, Philip was allowed to use an old **supercomputer** called the Connection Machine at the Los Alamos Laboratory in New Mexico. Los Alamos is a government research lab. From his base at the University of Michigan, he accessed the computer remotely, creating different **formulas** to improve the way computers work.

Through his work, Philip created a formula that allowed 65,000 microcomputers to perform 3.1 billion calculations per second.

This breakthrough allowed computers to talk to one another in record time. Philip had created the world's fastest computer. His discovery was important in the development of the Internet.

For his groundbreaking work, Philip has been called "the Bill Gates of Africa," after the famous American computer scientist and founder of Microsoft. Philip was awarded the Gordon Bell Prize for computing in 1989. It recognizes outstanding achievement in computer applications.

MARY SEACOLE

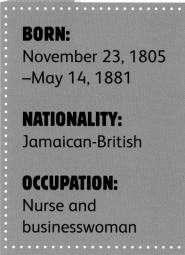

BORN:
November 23, 1805
–May 14, 1881

NATIONALITY:
Jamaican-British

OCCUPATION:
Nurse and
businesswoman

MISSION OF COMPASSION

Mary Seacole had already nursed British soldiers back to health in Jamaica, where she was born. When newspapers announced that many more British soldiers were dying from disease than from battle wounds during the **Crimean War**, Mary knew she had to help.

Mary learned half of her medical skills from her mother, a **traditional healer**, known as a "doctress" in Mary's hometown of Kingston, Jamaica. Doctresses used their knowledge of diseases, as well as Caribbean and African herbs, massage, and bonesetting techniques, to treat and heal people. The other half of Mary's skills were learned from watching and working with doctors and nurses at a home for injured soldiers and during her many travels.

In the autumn of 1854, Mary traveled from Jamaica to London to offer her services as an experienced nurse at the battlefronts of the Crimean War. It was the first major war where professional nurses were used. Mary was turned down by everyone. She wanted to work with Florence Nightingale, the founder of modern nursing. Again she was turned down. Many women were turned down because they lacked nursing skills or hospital experience, but Mary clearly had both. This led her to think that maybe her nursing skills were being rejected because of the color of her skin.

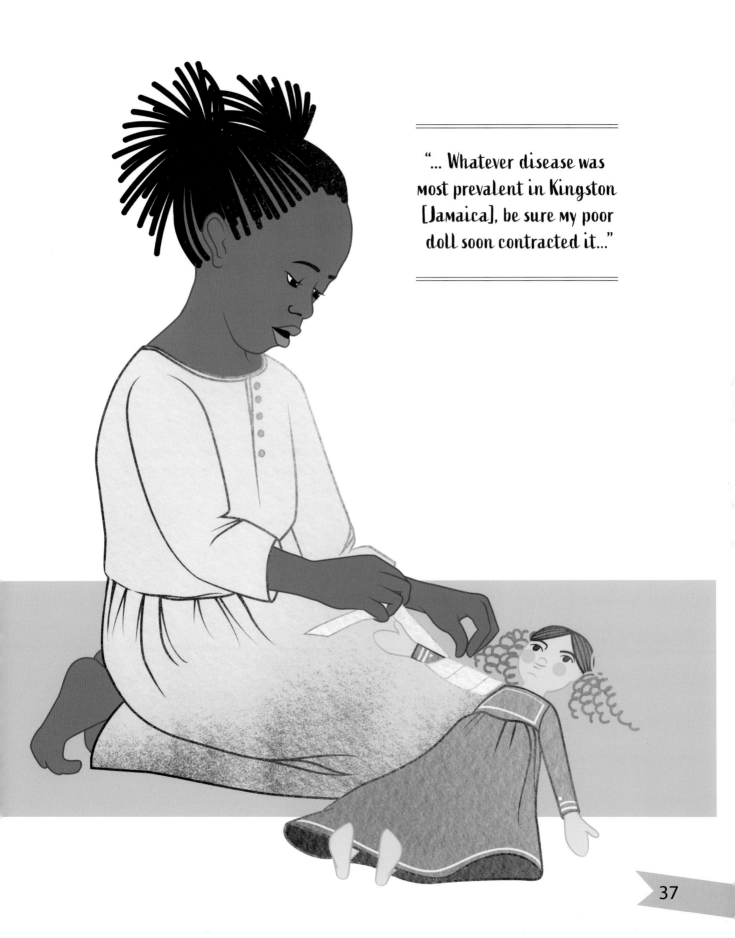

"... Whatever disease was most prevalent in Kingston [Jamaica], be sure my poor doll soon contracted it..."

> ## "Did these ladies shrink from accepting my aid because my blood flowed beneath a somewhat duskier skin than theirs?"

In October 1854, Florence Nightingale and her team of 38 nurses set off for Crimea in eastern Europe. But Mary was not among them. So she needed to find another way of reaching the Crimea. She decided to fund her own trip to the battlefields and she set off on her mission of compassion.

A plan took shape in Mary's mind. She planned to go to Balaklava in Crimea and set up a hotel for sick and injured British soldiers. She and a business partner would fund it themselves. They would sell hot meals, drinks, food and useful goods to army officers. The profits would pay for food and medicines for wounded men.

When Mary arrived in Balaklava, her supplies were limited. She had no building materials. So she gathered anything that looked like it could be useful from a neighboring village and she opened The British Hotel. It soon became popular with soldiers.

As well as running her business, Mary used her own money to buy medicines and food to give to wounded soldiers waiting to cross the sea to Scutari Hospital. There, Florence Nightingale and her nurses awaited them. She also rode a horse to visit sick soldiers in army camps and even nursed soldiers on the battlefields.

After the war ended in 1856, Mary returned to London in poor health and with little money. Her unselfish deeds in Crimea were remembered by the many soldiers she had helped. They set up a fund and raised money to help support Mary.

In 1857, Mary published her autobiography, *Wonderful Adventures of Mrs. Seacole in Many Lands*.

"... And the grateful words and smile which rewarded me for binding up a wound or giving a cooling drink was a pleasure worth risking life for at any time."

Read on to find out more about some other amazing Black scientists, both past and present.

DR. ALAN GOFFE

Alan Powell Goffe. Now there's an unsung hero! At a time when the deadly disease, **polio**, was affecting people around the world, Alan played a vital role in the development stages of a vaccine against it.

More importantly, Alan's work as a **microbiologist** in the 1950s and 1960s helped to make the polio vaccine safe to use for millions of people around the world. As a result, there was a huge decline in polio cases. Alan also helped to develop a breakthrough measles vaccine.

BORN:
July 9, 1920–
died August 13, 1966

NATIONALITY:
British-Jamaican

OCCUPATION:
Microbiologist/
virologist

DR. MARIE MAYNARD DALY

BORN:
April 16, 1921–
October 28, 2003

NATIONALITY:
American

OCCUPATION:
Biochemist

Marie Maynard Daly always knew what she wanted to be when she grew up: a chemist! It was a big dream for a little Black girl in the early 1900s. Her father's story was her inspiration. Although his own dream of being a chemist was cut short because he couldn't afford the university fees, Ivan Daly set the stage for his daughter to succeed.

Marie became the first African-American woman to receive a PhD in chemistry in the U.S. She is celebrated for her research on heart disease. Marie's work brought attention to how diet can affect the heart and **circulatory system** and is still relevant today.

DR. ERNEST EVERETT JUST

Ernest Everett Just was not a typical teenager. By age 15, he was qualified to teach. But teaching didn't interest Ernest. He studied for degrees in **Classics**, and then English, before being appointed as a professor at Howard University, in Washington, D.C.

Three years later Ernest was asked to run the biology department at Howard and his interest in science flourished. He decided to study for a PhD in biology alongside his new job as a researcher at Woods Hole Research Center in Massachusetts.

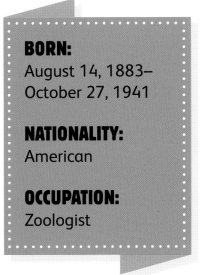

BORN:
August 14, 1883–
October 27, 1941

NATIONALITY:
American

OCCUPATION:
Zoologist

Ernest is best known for his research on marine invertebrates, which showed that an egg's surface plays an important role in its fertilization and development. Although the color of his skin kept him from working at most leading universities in his home country, his fame brought him work at research institutes in Italy and Germany. He was awared the National Association for the Advancement of Colored People's (NAACP) 1915 Springarn Medal for his contributions to science.

JESSE RUSSELL, SR.

Forty years ago, hardly anyone had a cell phone. Today, around five billion of the world's eight billion people have cell phones. Jesse Russell played a big part in putting cell phones into the hands of the people.

Although Martin Cooper invented the first mobile phone in 1973, Jesse came up with the idea of wireless phones. Before that time, mobile phones only worked through technology in people's cars. Jesse has made numerous innovations to improve wireless communications since the late 1980s. He has received many awards for his scientific and engineering inventions.

BORN:
April 26, 1948

NATIONALITY:
American

OCCUPATION:
Electrical engineer

CAROLYN PARKER

BORN:
November 18, 1917–
March 17, 1966

NATIONALITY:
American

OCCUPATION:
Physicist/professor

Some scientists risk their lives for their work. That's the story of Carolyn Parker, a physicist whose exposure to the chemical element polonium cut short her life and career.

Science success ran in the family for Carolyn. Her father was both a doctor and a pharmacist in Gainesville, Florida. All of her five siblings earned math, science, or social science degrees in university. Carolyn's first love was math, but, a lifelong learner and teacher, she earned degrees in physics as well.

As a young scientist during **World War II** (1939-45), Carolyn worked on the Dayton Project. This was a top-secret science lab that helped develop the atomic bomb. Dayton Project scientists worked with polonium which was used to kick-start the bomb's powerful chain reactions. Later, Carolyn became a professor at Fisk University, an historically Black college in Nashville, Tennessee. There, she taught the next generation of Black scientists while completing her PhD work. Carolyn died of leukemia, likely caused by the polonium she worked with earlier in her career.

DR. WANGARI MAATHAI

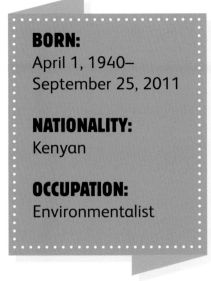

BORN:
April 1, 1940–
September 25, 2011

NATIONALITY:
Kenyan

OCCUPATION:
Environmentalist

Dr. Wangari Maathai was proof that just one person can make a big difference. As the first woman from East and Central Africa to be awarded a PhD, Wangari used her knowledge to help Kenyans.

After her studies, she became a professor at the University of Nairobi in Kenya. She became interested in finding ways to help rural women in Kenya. They were struggling to find fuel, water, and grow crops to feed their families. Wangari realized that the main problem was deforestation.

Wangari asked the women to join together to plant trees. This was the beginning of the Green Belt Movement, an organization dedicated to environmental conservation, reducing poverty, and defending human rights. Wangari then became involved with Kenyan politics, and held several important positions in government. In 2004, she became the first African woman to be awarded a **Nobel Prize**.

"We cannot tire or give up. We owe it to the present and future generations of all species to rise up and walk!"

DR. GLADYS WEST

Dr. Gladys West grew up in a small farming town in Virginia, where, after leaving school, most people worked on tobacco farms or in tobacco factories. Not Gladys. She wanted to do something different. She knew that getting a good education would be her only way out. So she worked hard at school and won a university scholarship. She chose to study math, a field studied mostly by men at that time.

After completing school, Gladys taught for a a few years and completed a Master's degree. She found work at the Naval Surface Warfare Center in Virginia, where she was only the second Black woman hired there. While working collecting data from satellites, Gladys completed another Master's degree. Her work eventually led to the development of **GPS (Global Positioning System)**. Without Gladys's contributions we would all be lost! Not one to rest, after retiring, Gladys completed a PhD– at age 88!

BORN:
c.1930

NATIONALITY:
American

OCCUPATION:
Mathematician

"You're always competing and trying to survive because you're in a different group of people."

DR. ANDERSON RUFFIN ABBOTT

BORN:
April 7, 1837–
December 29, 1913

NATIONALITY:
Canadian

OCCUPATION:
Physician/surgeon

It's not unusual for a father to want more for his children. Born a free Black man in Virginia, Anderson Ruffin Abbott's father, Wilson, left Alabama in 1834 when his business was threatened. He moved to Canada, and by 1840 was a successful businessman and member of city council in Toronto, Ontario. Still, he wanted his children to do even better.

His son Anderson Ruffin Abbott benefited from his father's wealth and standing, but he also worked hard to make his own name. As a child, Anderson's parents sent him to good schools in Canada and the United States. He attended the Toronto School of Medicine. In 1861, Anderson made history by becoming the first Canadian-born Black doctor.

Anderson volunteered to serve as a doctor to the Union side during the **Civil War** (1861–1865). He was at first rejected, but managed to serve as a surgeon. He later worked in American hospitals, where he was among the team of doctors who tried to save the life of the assassinated U.S. president, Abraham Lincoln.

After his return to Canada, Anderson set up practice in Chatham, Ontario, where he became president of the Chatham Medical Society and the local literary and debating society. He was also appointed **coroner** for Kent County, where Chatham is located. Anderson held many prominent positions in his life, including Medical Superintendent of Provident Hospital in Chicago in 1884. He was also president of Wilberforce Educational Institute from 1873-1880 and fought against segregation in schools.

GLOSSARY

agriculture The science behind growing crops and raising livestock

Apollo Program NASA's third human spaceflight program which ran from 1961 to 1972

arranged marriage A type of marital union where the bride and groom are chosen for each other by their parents

astronomy The study of the night sky, including the Sun, Moon, stars, and planets

circulatory system The organ system that permits blood to circulate in the body

Civil War (U.S.) A war (1861–1865) between the northern states (the Union) and southern states (the Confederacy) where the Union won

Classics The study of ancient Greek and Latin

conservationists People who protect the environment

coroner A doctor whose main job is to investigate the causes of deaths that are not clearly the result of natural causes

Crimean War A war fought by Britain, France, and Turkey against the Russian Empire between 1853 and 1856

custom The language, beliefs, music, art, and usual ways of doing things in a place

discrimination To treat a person or group of people better or worse than others, often because of their gender, race, or religion

dyslexia A learning disorder that makes it difficult for people to read

equation A way of solving a problem in math or science

famine Extreme scarcity of food that is usually the result of war or drought

fertile Able to produce many healthy crops

formula Letters, numbers, or symbols that represent a scientific or mathematical rule or law

GPS Global Positioning System, a worldwide navigational system that uses satellites in Earth's orbit to determine the location of something on Earth

inferiority To believe or consider something not as good or less than equal

injustice Something that is wrong or unfair

innovator Someone who makes something new or introduces new methods or ideas

intellectuals People who place a high value on knowledge and learning

microbiologist A scientist who studies micro-organisms such as bacteria and fungi

Nobel Prize An international prize awarded to recognize someone's work in their field

patent A protection granted by a government to an inventor, giving the inventor the right to stop others from making, using, or selling the invention, without permission

PhD Short for Doctor of Philosophy, a high-level university degree

polio An infectious disease that can cause paralysis and death

prejudice Hatred for, or unfair treatment of, a person or group of people without cause or reason

racial identification The race or group of people a person identifies with or feels they belong to

scalpel A small sharp knife used by doctors and vets to perform operations

scholarship An amount of money given to someone to help pay for their education

segregation The system of separating White people and Black people in order to deny Black people equal opportunities in education, health, housing, and other areas

sterilize To clean something using alcohol or boiling water and remove the germs that could cause disease

supercomputer A computer with a high level of performance often used for scientific or engineering applications

surveyor Someone who measures and records the size and shape of a piece of land

traditional healer A person, usually from an Indigenous or other group, who practices the art of traditional remedies and methods of healing disease using plants and minerals

vaccine A special substance that protects a person against a disease

World War II A war that broke out in Europe and spread around the world during 1939–1945

LEARNING MORE

Books

Brown Pellum, Kimberley. *Black Women in Science*. Rockridge Press, 2019.

Cooke, Tim. *Working Toward Achieving Civil Rights*. Crabtree Publishing, 2020.

Walker, Robin. *Black History Matters*. Franklin Watts, 2019.

Wilson, Jamia. *Young, Gifted, and Black*. Wide-Eyed Editions, 2018.

Websites and videos

Discover some of **George Washington Carver's** amazing peanut inventions at: **tuskegee.edu/support-tu/george-washington-carver/carver-peanut-products**

Learn more about **Mae Jemison's** space story at: **www.youtube.com/watch?v=tCMJW-auEhE**

Find out more about **Mary Seacole** at: **www.maryseacoletrust.org.uk**

The website addresses (URLs) included in this book were valid at the time of printing. It is possible that contents or addresses may have changed since the publication of this book. Neither the Publisher or author accept responsibility for any changes.

QUOTE SOURCES

Benjamin Banneker: p.8: "I freely and cheerfully…" www.blackthen.com/benjamin-bannekers-1791-letter-thomas-jefferson-jeffersons-reply/. **Segenet Kelumu**: p.10: "If you don't have food…" Gates, Bill. "No Mask or Caps, But these Heroes Are Saving the World" Gates Notes Blog. January 4, 2018. Digital/Video; p.10: "As I was handed…" VPRO Documentary. "Dreams that Inspired Great Discoveries" Video, Youtube. **Dr. Maggie Aderin-Pocock**: p.13: "My problem with education…" Armstrong, Simon, "New Sky at Night Presenter," BBC, December 13, 2013. Digital; p.14: "Every night they opened…" The Royal Institute, "Ri Unconference: Maggie Aderin-Pocock - Science and Careers," December 8, 2011. Digital. **George Washington Carver**: p.17: "Where the soil…" Iowa Public Television, "George Washington Carver: An Uncommon Life," May 8, 2028. Digital. **Dr. Mae Jemison**: p.19: "I always believed…" Keoghan, Phil, "BUCKit #15: Mae Jemison: First Female African American Astronaut," September 26, 2018. Digital; p.21: "I didn't even think about…" Nova's Secret Life of Scientist and Engineers," Mae Jemison: "I Wanted to Go Into Space," July 31, 2014. Digital. **Drs. Mamie & Kenneth Clark**: p.23: "They were emotionally upset…" CSPAN, "Landmark Cases: Brown vs Board Doll Test," November 23, 2015. Digital. **Dr. Patricia Bath** p.25: "Eyesight is a basic right." Good Morning America, "Meet a Woman Who Changed the Face of Medicine," February 26,

2018. Digital. www.youtube.com/watch?v=HTRuxm15dxM. p.27 "It's only when history…" Time, "Patricia Bath on Being the First Person to Invent & Demonstrate Laserphaco Cataract Surgery," October 30, 2017. Digital. www.youtube.com/watch?v=gcE_QMTBNW4. p.28: "I did not allow…" Good Morning America, "Meet a Woman Who Changed the Face of Medicine," February 26, 2018. Digital. www.youtube.com/watch?v=HTRuxm15dxM. **Dr. Daniel Hale Williams**: p.32: "A people who don't…" www.columbiasurgery.org. **Philip Emeagwali**: p.34: "It is smarter…" Bellis, Mary, "The Life of Philip Emeagwali-Supercomputers," The Inventors.org, Digital. **Mary Seacole**: p.37: "Whatever disease…" Seacole, Mary and Sara Salih, "Wonderful Adventures of Mrs. Seacole In Many Lands," Penguin Classics, November 29, 2005; p.38: "Did these ladies…" Seacole, Mary and Sara Salih, "Wonderful Adventures of Mrs. Seacole In Many Lands," Penguin Classics, November 29, 2005; "…And the grateful words…" Seacole, Mary and Sara Salih, "Wonderful Adventures of Mrs. Seacole In Many Lands," Penguin Classics, November 29, 2005. **Dr. Wangari Maathai**: p.43: "We cannot tire…" www.greenbeltmovement.org. **Dr. Gladys West**: p.44: "You're always competing…" Butterfly, Amelia "100 Women: Gladys West – The Hidden Figure of GPS" BBC News, May 20, 2018.

INDEX

AUTHOR AND ILLUSTRATOR BIOGRAPHIES

In *Black Stories Matter: Groundbreaking Scientists*, you will read the stories of Black scientists and inventors from around the world. These brave and ingenious men and women pushed against laws and stereotypes. They are only a few of the many who have had an impact on the world with their scientific discoveries.

J.P. Miller is a children's author with an interest in the African Diaspora. She hopes that her stories will set fire to old stereotypes and shed light on the many contributions Black people have made throughout the world. J.P lives in Metro Atlanta, Georgia.

Chellie Carroll is an artist who shares her time with her two children, climbing crags and hills near her home in Derbyshire, U.K.